DID YOU KNOW?
The Rainbow Edition

Written and Illustrated by Sherry Stone Yetter

Did You Know? The Rainbow Edition
published by Sunflower Books LLC.
www.sunflowerbooksllc.com
ISBN: 978-1-7358619-0-6 (paperbook)
First Edition, 2020
Text copyright © Sherry Stone Yetter 2020
Illustration copyright © Sherry Stone Yetter 2020

Written by Sherry Stone Yetter
Illustrations by Sherry Stone Yetter
Edited/Designed by Gregg Yetter

Special acknowledgements to my loving husband Gregg;
to Traci for encouraging me to follow my dreams;
to Clarissa and Brandon for being my inspiration; and,
last but not least, to my family and friends who have
always believed in me.

****

Illustrations were created using Canva.. Thank you: clairev, icons8, Artner Dluxe, Joy image, Notion Pic, sketchify, pixabay, DAPA images, djvstock2 , oleksa, PavelVectors, Aurielaki, vectortradition, vintageillustrations, printablepretty, BNPdesignstudio, iconsy, jemastock, studiog, eyewave, Victoria Sergeeva, GeoImages, cuttlefish, yayayoyo, DKDesignz, Nataliya Yakovleva, Buch&Bee, lineartestpilot, Marco Livolsi, Yupiramos, Allies Interactive, ivandesign, smalllike, alexanderkonoplyov, gstudioimagen2, Andres Rodriguez, lastspark, Marketplace Designers, marynaalokina, Phoebe Yu.

9 781735 861906

This book is dedicated to the littles in my life
– Jody, Phoebe, and Levi –
You are my heart

Happy 3rd Birthday Phoebe

LOVE, GIGI

Did You Know?

A rainbow forms because of the sun and the rain.

Did You Know?

    A rainbow forms when the sun's rays reflect itself through thousands of tiny droplets of water.

Did You Know?

    A rainbow is a curved line of color seen in the sky when the sun shines through the rain.

Did You Know?

A rainbow forms a full circle but we only see part of it. The part we see is in the shape of an arch or a half-circle.

Did You Know?
The colors of a rainbow are red, orange, yellow, green, blue, indigo, and violet.

Did You Know? The color R E D ...

can be seen from far distances,

is a color that shows love,

can be seen by monkeys, squirrels, birds, and fish,

and is used to indicate 'STOP'.

 Can you name all the red objects?

Did You Know? The color O R A N G E ...

is the only color named after a fruit,

does not rhyme with any other
English word,

can easily be seen in low light,

and is often used on safety items.

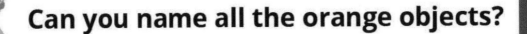

Can you name all the orange objects?

Did You Know? The color YELLOW ...

is the color of the sun,

makes us feel warm,

is bright and cheerful,

and is a color of happiness.

Can you name all the yellow objects?

Did You Know? The color G R E E N ...

is a color often seen in nature,

is used to indicate 'GO',

is considered a
lucky color,

and is the world's second
favorite color.

Can you name the green objects?

Did You Know? The color B L U E ...

makes you feel calm,

is the color of Earth's
    sky, seas, and oceans,

is a color to show coldness,

and is the world's favorite color.

Can you name all the blue objects?

Did You Know? The color I N D I G O ...

originated in India,

is a shade of blue,

is named after a plant,

and is green until air changes the
color.

Can you name all the indigo objects?

Did You Know? The color V I O L E T ...

is the seventh color of the rainbow,

is a shade of purple,

and is named after a small,
pretty flower.

Can you name all
the violet objects?

Did You Know?

We are learning about science.

Rainbows and colors
are super fun to read about.

Now, let's learn some more fun facts.

Did You Know?

Sir Isaac Newton is a scientist who discovered the seven different colors in a rainbow.

You cannot touch a rainbow.

A rainbow moves as you move.

Rainbows are a sign of peace and harmony.

Sometimes one raindrop will reflect the sun twice to create a double rainbow.

Rainbows that happen at night are called moonbows.

Did You Know?

The colors red, yellow, and blue
are called primary colors.

The color green is between yellow
and blue on a rainbow.

The color orange is created when
you add two colors together.

Did You Know?

Each color in a rainbow decreases
in brightness and eventually
blend together.

When colors blend together
we create new ones like orange
and green and purple and violet.

Check out the next page and
learn how to create three new colors.

Red + Blue = Purple

Blue + Yellow = Green

Red + Yellow = Orange

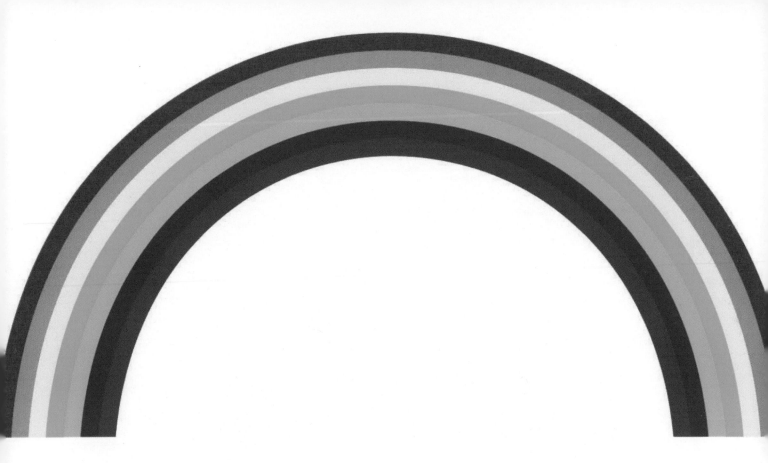

Did You Know?

Rainbows and bright, vibrant colors go together like paint and paper or chocolate and milk.

When we mix things together we create new things which is fun!

Can you color a rainbow? I bet you can. Go ahead and give it a try.

My Rainbow

ABOUT THE AUTHOR

Sherry Yetter is the author of new series of children's books titled "*Did You Know?*" that will teach and entertain even the youngest of readers. "*Did You Know? The Rainbow Edition*" is the first book published in this series. Sherry and her husband (a U.S. Marine) are currently stationed at MCB Quantico, VA but they call Kansas City, MO home. Sherry is a Mom, Gigi, and a fur baby Mom to a spunky Havanese and a loving rescue named Jozie. Sherry has dedicated her life to to serving others, leading organizations, and helping service-members and military families build family centered resiliency. Sherry is currently devoting her time to writing and building communities of hope, justice, and kindness.

This is Sherry's first published book.